100 Things You R Need to Know

According to Bill Condon
Illustrated by Terry Denton

CELEBRATION PRESS
Pearson Learning Group

The ten things you really must know!

1 Whether you are a boy or a girl. (If you're not sure, ask your parents.)

2 Your address. (It will take a long time to get home without knowing this.)

3 How to program the VCR or the DVD. (Your parents won't be able to figure this out, so it's up to you!)

4 The date of your birthday. (People need to put a lot of thought into this. So, if, for example, your birthday is on May 1st, you should start dropping hints about your next birthday on May 2nd.)

5 The birthdays of your family and friends. (Being kind to others will make you feel good too.)

6　What parents most hate hearing from kids when they're in the car: "Are we there yet?"

7　What kids most hate hearing from parents when they're in the car: "We just passed the last rest room . . . it's only two more hours before the next one."

8　The worst excuse for not doing your homework: "I had too much TV to watch!"

9　Green vegetables are not as bad as they look . . . they're worse! (Only kidding! They're good for you. That's why Superman can leap tall buildings in a single bean.)

10　Your parents were once the same age as you! (And they were probably just as naughty.)

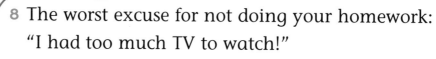

Fantastic facts

Babies and birthdays

11 About four babies are born every second.

12 Your birthday is shared by about 9 million other people. (Don't even think about sending them all birthday cards.)

13 Babies have been known to hiccup several hours before birth—sometimes very loudly.

14 It takes most babies two years before they can put two or three words together.

15 Babies are born without kneecaps. They don't appear until the baby is between two and six months old.

16 The most popular names for baby boys are Michael, Jacob, Matthew, and Christopher. (The least popular is Lumpy.)

17 In Russia, many children are given a birthday pie instead of a birthday cake.

18 A Russian woman gave birth to 69 children. She had 16 pairs of twins, seven sets of triplets, and four sets of quadruplets. They all lived, except for two.

19 Many Korean and Mongolian babies are born with a blue spot on their lower backs. It disappears after a couple of years.

20 People spend one-third of their lives asleep.

21 It takes about seven minutes for most people to get to sleep.

22 Children grow the most when they are asleep.

23 Dolphins sleep with one eye open.

24 Lions can sleep for up to 20 hours a day.

25 Ants never sleep.

26 Horses can go to sleep standing up.

Body bits

27 A sneeze travels faster than a speeding car.

28 It is impossible to sneeze with your eyes open.

29 Every month you grow a brand new layer of skin.

30 Water makes up more than half of our body content.

31 When you blink an eye you move more than 200 muscles.

32 The average person walks the equivalent of twice around the world in their lifetime.

33 Everyone's fingerprints are different. (And no two cows, or giraffes, have the same pattern of spots, either.)

34 If you ate too many carrots you'd turn orange!

35 The only animal that can smile is a human being. (So what are you waiting for? Smile!)

36 Eskimos kiss by rubbing noses together.

37 The average human body contains enough: sulfur to kill all the fleas on an average dog; potassium to fire a toy cannon; carbon to make 900 pencils; fat to make seven bars of soap; 9 gallons of water; and phosphorus to make 2,200 match heads.

38 It takes Asian elephants more than twice as long as humans to have babies—about 20 months.

39 A cow produces about 200,000 glasses of milk during her life. (And none of it is chocolate flavored!)

40 The bird-eating spider of north Queensland is Australia's biggest spider. (It has been known to drag live chickens away to eat.)

41 Australia's koala "bears" are not really bears. They are marsupials. (They're really called *koalas*.)

42 Chickens can't swallow if held upside down.

43 Baby goats have the same name as children—they are called *kids*.

44 Zebras are white, with black stripes.

45 A camel can drink 47 gallons of water at one time. (That's equal to about 495 cans of soft drink.)

46 The American horned toad squirts blood from its eyes.

47 Some blue whales weigh more than the largest dinosaurs did.

48 The only dogs that don't bark are the Basenjis. (And all dogs have pink tongues—except the chow.)

49 The world's smallest dog is the Chihuahua, which means "tiny dog in the sky."

50 The heaviest dog is the St. Bernard. It can weigh almost 200 pounds.

51 Kangaroos are about the size of a peanut when they are born.

52 Africa's cheetah is the fastest land animal—it can run at 60 miles per hour.

53 The bee hummingbird is the smallest bird in the world.

54 The ostrich is the tallest bird in the world. It weighs as much as 48,000 bee hummingbirds.

55 The longest-living animal is the giant tortoise of the Galapagos Islands. Some have lived for 190 years.

56 The oldest age to which any human has lived is 122 years. She was Jeanne Louise Calment, 1875–1997, from France.

57 The world's tallest person was American Robert Wadlow. He was 8 feet 10 inches tall. Basketball player Michael Jordan is 6 feet 6 inches tall.

58 More people live in China than in any other country.

59 The youngest Pope was 11 years old.

60 Tutankhamun became Egypt's pharoah (or king) when he was only nine.

61 The largest volcano known to humans is on the planet Mars. It is three times higher than Mount Everest, Earth's tallest mountain.

62 In 1956, there was an iceberg in the South Pacific larger than Belgium.

63 Gorillas beat their chest when they are nervous.

YUK!

64 Cats get fur balls in their stomachs from licking themselves.

65 The bristles of the first toothbrushes were made from a pig's hair.

HEY, DAD! IS THIS YOUR HAIR ON MY TOOTHBRUSH?

66 A baby rattlesnake is just as deadly as its mom or dad.

67 A fox's tail is called a *brush*.

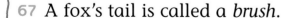

68 A camel can go without water for almost a week. (But to be healthy, *you* need water every day.)

69 Rats last longer without water than camels.

70 The female lion does more than 90 percent of the hunting, while the male is afraid to risk his life, or simply prefers to rest.

71 An octopus has three hearts.

THE EXTINCT PIRANHA BIRD.

72 A two-day-old gazelle can run faster than a horse.

73 Frogs and mosquitoes have teeth, but birds don't.

74 Japanese people love to eat raw fish, which is called *sushi*.

75 Russians love to eat borsch, a soup made from beet roots.

76 In South Africa, termites are roasted and eaten by the handful, like popcorn.

77 The sunfish can produce the most eggs of any fish—up to 300 million at one time.

78 Piranhas, fish from South America, eat other animals alive.

I DON'T FEEL WELL!

79 Sharks cannot swim backwards.

80 Fish can get seasick if kept on board a ship.

81 If goldfish are kept in running water they lose their color.

82 The archer fish can shoot a stream of water out of its mouth to knock bugs into the water and eat them.

83 The tongue of a blue whale is as long as an elephant.

84 Most butterflies only live for one month.
(Some live for only one day.)

85 A housefly lives only 14 days.

86 One queen termite can produce over 500 million offspring.

87 Bees have to visit about 5,000 flowers to make just one spoonful of honey.

88 The darkling beetle does a handstand; then squirts a bad-smelling liquid at animals it doesn't like.

89 Bombardier beetles squirt boiling water at animals they don't like.

90 There is a bird that barks instead of sings. It is the size of a duck but wasn't discovered until 1998 in Ecuador.

91 The hummingbird is the only bird that can fly backwards or hover in the same spot, like a helicopter.

92 Canada's national sport is lacrosse. It was first played by Native Americans who sometimes had as many as 1,000 men on each side.

THAT IS MY SON OUT THERE.

93 An American once dropped his watch from a plane then found it later in his own backyard. The watch still worked!

...AND... ACTION!!

94 A movie called *Sleep* runs for eight hours—and the whole time it shows a man sleeping.

95 An ancient cure for toothache was to eat a mouse. (But what if a mouse had a toothache?)

96 Someone once invented an alarm clock that woke sleepers by pouring cold water over them.

97 A woman named Constance Honey invented a spoon to help children swallow yucky medicine. The spoon was made of chocolate.

98 Italian Leonardo Da Vinci, who painted the world's most famous portrait—the "Mona Lisa"—made drawings of tanks, parachutes and helicopters 500 years before they were invented. (Leonardo could also write with one hand and draw with the other at the same time!)

99 In 1931 a poodle named Toby became the richest dog in the world when its owner left it $169 million in his will.

100 Each January in Queensland, Australia, the world championship of cockroach racing is held.